SENSELESS

Take part in a sensational interactive adventure!

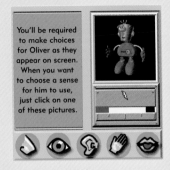

You'll be required to make choices for Oliver as they appear on screen. When you want to choose a sense for him to use, just click on one of these pictures.

Help! Oliver has been kidnapped and he needs you to help him escape. Use your knowledge of the senses to guide Oliver through the game. Stay alert for the hidden clues along the way.

TOP TO TOE

Here's your chance to put the senses to the test!

Meet Sensitive Sam and discover how his senses respond to the items on screen. Examine his body with your mouse and put each of his senses to the test.

FACE FACTS

Are you ready to face up to this challenging quiz?

Try this quiz to see if your knowledge of the senses is up to scratch. Can you get enough correct answers to put some sense back into Susan's face?

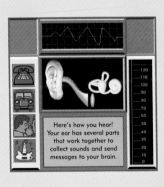

HEAR HEAR

Sound off to learn about hearing!

Here's how you hear! Your ear has several parts that work together to collect sounds and send messages to your brain.

Spend some time at the sound factory and discover how the ear works. Experiment with different sounds to learn all about decibels and frequency.

What's in the book

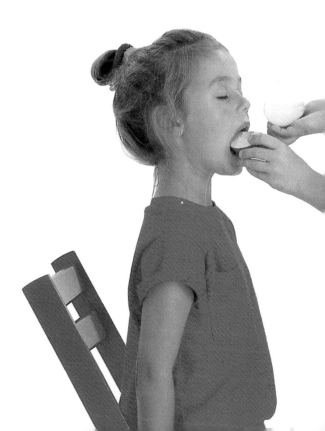

INTERFACT ™

THE BOOK AND DISK THAT WORK TOGETHER

SENSES

03216

03216

Created and published by
Two-Can Publishing Ltd
346 Old Street
London
EC1V 9NQ

Disk
Creative Director: William Wharfe
Programming Director: Paul Steven
Art Director: Sarah Evans
Designer: James Evans
Editor: Lyndall Thomas
Programmers: Craig Grummitt,
Colette McFadden, Roger Emery
Consultant: Graham Peacock
Illustrators: Michele Egar, Jon Stuart,
James Jarvis, Carlo Tartaglia
Production Director: Lorraine Estelle
Project Manager: Joya Bart-Plange

Book
Creative Director: William Wharfe
Editor: Lyndall Thomas
Author: Monica Byles
Designer: Michele Egar
Photography: Paul Bricknell, Toby Maudsley
Consultant: Graham Peacock
Production Director: Lorraine Estelle
Project Manager: Joya Bart-Plange

MAC ISBN 1-85434-505-2
PC ISBN 1-85434-501-X
CD ISBN 1-85434-509-5

Dewey Decimal Classification 612.8

2 4 6 8 10 9 7 5 3

A catalogue record for this book is available from the British Library

Printed in Hong Kong by Wing King Tong

Photographic Credits: Front cover: Tony Stone Images
Bruce Coleman: p15 tr; p23; p24 tr; p29 tr;
Hutchison: p20 b; p21 t; p 30 cl;
ZEFA: p9 t; p9 bl; p11 t; p12 c; p13 tl; p14 tr; p 17 tr;
Guide Dogs for the Blind Association: p 33
Illustrations by Nancy Anderson

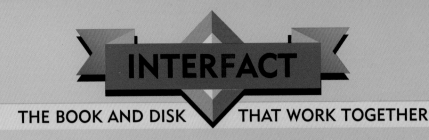

INTERFACT

THE BOOK AND DISK THAT WORK TOGETHER

INTERFACT will have you hooked in minutes –
and that's a fact!

🔵 The disk is packed with interactive
activities, puzzles, quizzes and games
that are great fun
to do and full of
interesting facts.

The nutty professor is
here to help you with
any of your questions
about the senses.

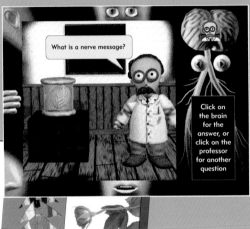

🔵 Open the
book and discover
more fascinating
information
highlighted with
lots of full-colour
illustrations and
photographs.

Read up about
the way your
senses help you
to understand the
world around you.

🔵 To get the most out of **INTERFACT**,
use the book and disk together.
Look out for the special signs,
called Disk Links and Bookmarks.
To find out more, turn to page 43.

23

BOOKMARK

DISK LINK
Take your
senses on
an adventure
when you
play SENSELESS.

Once you've clicked on to
INTERFACT, you'll never
look back.

LOAD UP!
Go to **page 40** to find out how to load
your disk and click into action.

What's on the disk

HELP SCREEN

Learn how to use the disk in no time at all.

Get to grips with the controls and find out how to use:
- arrow keys
- reading boxes
- 'hot' words

EYE OPENERS

You won't believe your eyes once you have seen these optical illusions!

Learn all about vision as you take a close look at these optical tricks. You can even have a go at creating some illusions of your own. You'll find more than meets the eye!

GREY MATTER

Put some of your brain power to use!

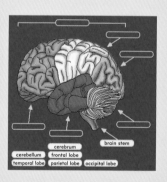

See if you can label the parts of the human brain. Then, click on each part to find out more. You'll learn about the control centres for each of the senses.

MAKING SENSE

Ask the experts for the information that you've been looking for!

Meet the nutty professor and his brainy friend! They've got the necessary know-how to answer all of your questions about the senses.

*All words in the text that appear in **bold** can be found in the glossary*

What are the senses?

When you wake up in the morning do you feel the warmth of your bed, switch off the alarm, look around the room, listen for sounds in the house and sniff for breakfast?

All of these actions involve your senses. People have five senses that receive messages from the world around them: sight, hearing, smell, touch and taste. These messages provide us with useful information, such as whether a situation is dangerous, if food is available, or how close or far away things are.

DISK LINK
What about hunger or thirst? Find out about the internal senses in MAKING SENSE.

Your senses also give you information about things that are attractive in the environment around you, such as bright colours or beautiful scents. Bright colours are often used in advertising to make products attractive to customers. In the natural world, bright colours may have developed for display purposes, or to act as a warning.

Can you work out which senses the pictures on these pages represent? (Two pictures show touch).

Busy messengers

Your eyes, ears, tongue, nose and skin are working all the time, receiving information from the world around you. Even as you sleep, they send signals to your **brain**.

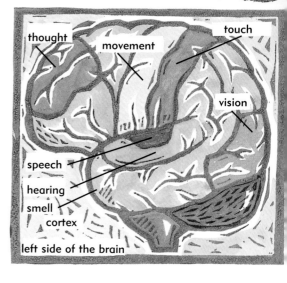

thought

movement

touch

vision

speech

hearing

smell

cortex

left side of the brain

▲ Your brain is made up of billions of tiny **cells**. The wrinkly, outer layer of the brain is called the **cortex**. Messages from your tongue, eyes, ears, nose and skin pass along **nerves** to special areas of the cortex, each concerned with a particular sense.

▼ As you look at these strawberries, a message travels from your eyes to your brain. The brain sends signals to the rest of your body, then your mouth starts to water and you begin to feel hungry.

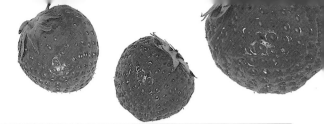

▼ Young puppies cannot see properly so they use their strong sense of smell to nuzzle their way to their mother's milk.

DISK LINK
You can take a closer look at each of the parts of the brain in GREY MATTER.

▶ Take care before touching hot things. When you touch something hot, your brain receives an alarm message from the nerve endings in your skin. Your brain will quickly tell your **muscles** to pull your hand away if an object is hot enough to hurt you.

Sight

Only a small part of your eye can be seen from the outside of your body. Your eyeball is actually the size of a ping-pong ball, set back into your skull. Your eyelids, eyelashes and eyebrows keep dirt out of your eyes. Every few seconds, your eyelids blink, covering your eyes with a salty fluid. This helps to keep your eyeballs moist and removes any dirt or dust that gets in.

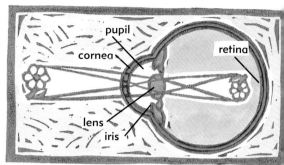

▲ An image is made up of light reflected from an object. As your eyes receive light, it passes through the **cornea** and enters the **pupil**. The light then passes through a **lens**, which turns the image upside down and brings it into **focus** on the light-sensitive cells of the **retina**. These cells send the upside down image to the brain. The image is turned up the right way by the brain.

▲ Your two eyes see things from slightly different angles. The brain joins the two images together and judges depth and distance. This makes a '3-D' picture. Chameleons can swivel their eyes around in their sockets, or even turn one eye forwards and the other eye backwards. Chameleons can see in two directions at the same time, which helps them to watch out for danger.

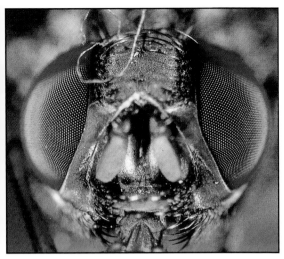

◀ Hawks use their excellent eyesight to spot prey moving on the ground far below.

◀ A fly's eye is made up of thousands of tiny lenses, each one facing a different direction. The fly's brain sees an image in pieces, rather than as a single picture.

▲ Make some cardboard spectacles. Cut one red lens and one green lens from coloured acetate. Draw pictures in red and green and look at them through the spectacles. Close one eye, then the other. What happens to the pictures?

◀ Put a variety of objects on a tray. Ask a friend to look at the objects for two minutes, then cover the tray with a cloth. How many things can your friend still remember? Now you try. Who can remember more objects?

Dark and bright

The pupil is the tiny hole in the front of the eye. The coloured **iris** changes the size of the pupil. This controls the light that enters the eye. In dim light the pupil gets larger and in bright light it gets smaller.

▲ Giraffes have good eyesight to watch out for danger over long distances.

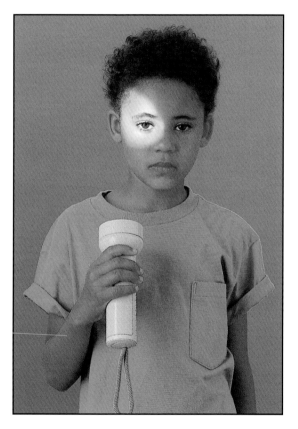

▲ Turn off the light and draw the curtains in a room. Point a torch so that a little light falls near the face of a friend. Look at one of your friend's eyes. How big is the pupil? Shine the torch closer to the eye. Does the pupil grow bigger or smaller? Now look at the other eye. Has the pupil of this eye changed size?

▶ Cats can see much better in the dark than people. At night, their large pupils widen so that the reflective layers at the back of their eyes can receive extra light. In bright sunlight, a cat's pupils close to form narrow slits.

DISK LINK
Have a go at playing some more tricks on your eyes in **EYE OPENERS**.

◀ Draw or paint a shape with thick black lines on plain white paper. Stare at it for at least one minute. Now close your eyes tightly. What do you see? For a short while, your brain will hold on to a reverse of the image, white on black, rather like the negative of a photograph.

Smell

You use your nose to breathe air in and out. Your nose is very sensitive and can detect many different smells from the air that you breathe in.

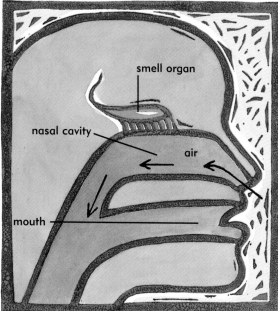

smell organ

nasal cavity

air

mouth

▲ When you sniff, air is sucked into your nose. It passes over the tiny hairs that line the nasal cavity and trap any dirt or dust. When the air reaches the back of the nose, it passes over a **membrane** that is packed with nerves. The nerves send signals to the brain and these are interpreted as smells.

▼ How well can you smell? Blindfold a friend and ask her to identify different foods and flowers by sniffing them. You could try orange juice, ginger, mustard and lavender. Can she tell them apart? Now, mix two of them together.

DISK LINK
How does Sensitive Sam's nose react to nice smells and nasty ones? Find out in TOP TO TOE.

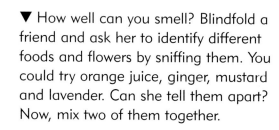

Can your friend still tell which is which? Who is the best sniffer in your group of friends? Other things you could include in the smell test are slices of cucumber, lemon, roses, cheese, carrots, garlic or curry powder.

▲ These Arctic wolves have long, large noses. Many types of dog have noses that are one million times more sensitive than a person's nose, so they can detect smells that most people would not notice. A powerful sense of smell helps wild dogs find food and distinguish between friends and enemies.

Scent and savour

Some people, such as wine tasters, use their sense of smell at work. Perfume makers can tell up to 10,000 different smells apart. But with a cold, even they would find it hard to smell because the nose becomes blocked with **mucus**.

DISK LINK
Get a whiff of this! These pages contain clues that will help you when you play SENSELESS.

Pleasant scents are often added to perfume, bath oil, foods and stationery to make them more appealing. Some scents are made artificially but many are made from natural sources, such as flower petals. Other scents are used to repel. For example, moths keep well away from fabrics stored with moth balls.

▲ Have you ever noticed how bad food smells when it begins to rot? This is nature's way of warning you not to eat food that could make you ill. **Bacteria** start to grow on old food and break it down, releasing the bad odour. You may see signs of mould too.

◄ Make a scratch and sniff card. Draw a shape on a piece of card and then glue all sorts of smelly herbs, spices or talc on to different areas of the drawing. It should look quite colourful. Can your friends tell which substances you used by sniffing the card? You could use the card for a special friend's birthday.

Taste

Your tongue has two important jobs to do. It helps you to shape words so that you can talk. But it also allows you to taste and eat food. It sorts and shapes food as you chew and swallow.

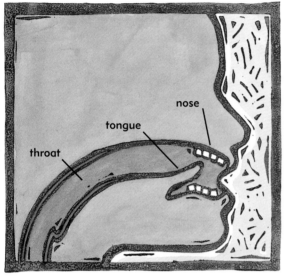

nose

tongue

throat

▲ When you chew and swallow food, your mouth produces a liquid, called **saliva**. It is released by the **glands** in your tongue and cheeks, and mixes with the food in your mouth to make a smooth, wet paste. Saliva also starts to **digest**, or break down, the food.

▶ Do you like eating seafood, such as mussels? Across the world, people enjoy eating a huge variety of different foods. Aboriginals in Australia love fat, white wichety grubs, which they eat fresh or roasted over a fire. Other delicacies people eat include chocolate-covered insects, such as locusts and grasshoppers, dried seaweed, frog's legs, snails and snakes. Which food tastes best to you?

▼ These sticks of edible clay are eaten by some of the local people of Nigeria. The clay is a valuable source of calcium in their diet. Calcium is a **mineral** that your body uses to make your teeth and bones strong. Everyone needs to eat a balanced mixture of minerals, vitamins, fats, fibre and carbohydrates to stay healthy.

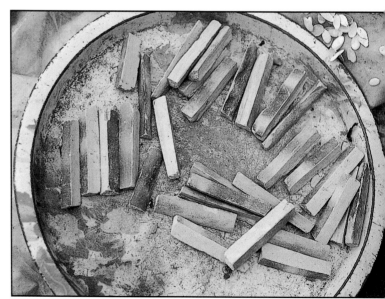

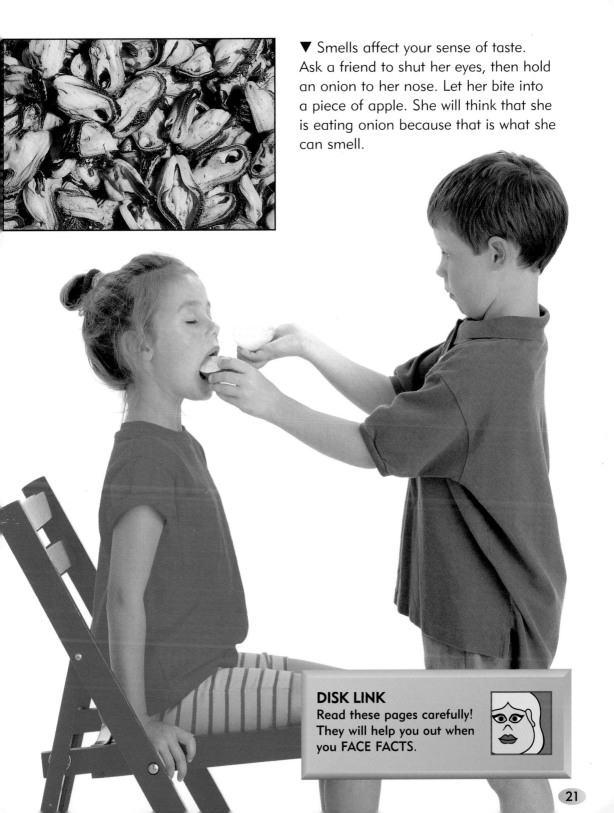

▼ Smells affect your sense of taste. Ask a friend to shut her eyes, then hold an onion to her nose. Let her bite into a piece of apple. She will think that she is eating onion because that is what she can smell.

DISK LINK
Read these pages carefully! They will help you out when you **FACE FACTS**.

Sweet and sour

When you eat or drink, your sense of taste and your sense of smell are working at the same time to distinguish between the different flavours.

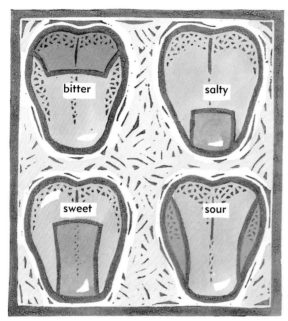

▲ Your tongue is covered with about 3,000 taste buds. These are tiny hollows in the tongue's surface, lined with taste-sensitive cells. There are four main types of taste: sweet, bitter, salty and sour. Some groups of buds are better than others at sensing each type of taste. The buds send messages along the nerves to the taste centre in the brain.

▼ The colour of food may make it more or less appealing to you. Put drops of different food dyes into glasses of fruit juice. Can your friends spot each flavour, or are they put off by the colouring?

► A toad extends its tongue to lick up an earwig. Its tongue can flick out and back again in one-tenth of a second.

▲ A hummingbird has a very long, thin tongue and beak to reach the sugary nectar inside a flower. The nectar contains lots of sugar and tastes very sweet. This provides hummingbirds with the energy that they need to keep their hearts and wings beating rapidly.

Touch

Hot, cold, wet, dry, soft or prickly: the nerve endings in your skin are constantly giving your brain information about the conditions of your body and the world around you.

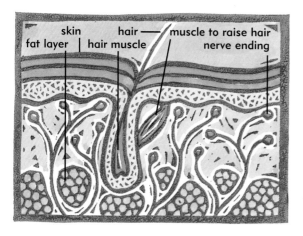

▲ A fly triggers touch-sensitive hairs on a Venus flytrap. The leaves close to trap the fly, ready for the plant to digest.

▲ Skin is a thin layer covering your whole body. Just beneath the surface of your skin there are nerve endings that send messages to your brain about touch, temperature and pain. When you are hot, your skin produces **sweat** to cool you down. And when you are cold, the tiny hairs on your skin rise to trap a layer of warm air around you. Every day, millions of cells are lost from the surface of your skin. Your body is constantly making new cells to replace them. Your skin is stretchy and it moves and grows with your body.

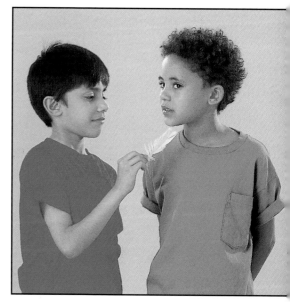

▲ Tickle a friend with a feather. Which areas of skin are the most sensitive?

▼ Every single person in the world has a unique pattern of tiny ridges on their finger tips, called a fingerprint. The police use fingerprint records to help track down suspects. Keep a file of the fingerprints of your family and friends. Press each finger tip on a stamp pad, then on to paper. Label each set of prints so that you know who they belong to.

▲ The colour of your skin depends on how much **melanin** it contains. People with white skin have very little melanin. After a few days in the sun, their skin produces more melanin and develops a tan. People with darker skin have a lot of melanin.

25

Hot and cold

The nerve endings that tell your brain about touch, temperature or pain are in groups beneath the surface of your skin. Some areas of your skin are packed with one type of nerve ending, so they are more sensitive to that type of feeling.

DISK LINK
How does your body sense temperature? The professor will help you to find the answer in MAKING SENSE.

▲ Do you dip your toes into the bath to test the temperature before you get in? The nerve endings in your toes are very sensitive to hot and cold.

◄ Try to identify objects by touch. Make a hole in a box and put some objects with different textures inside, such as a sponge or jelly. Ask your friends to put their hand into the box. Can they name each object?

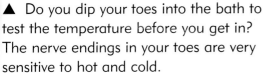

▲ See how cold things affect your sense of touch. Put your fingers in a bowl of melting ice cubes for about 30 seconds. Now touch something very soft and then something prickly. What do you feel? The cold of the ice cubes numbs your nerve endings so they do not send accurate signals to your brain.

Do not touch ice straight from the freezer, as it could hurt your skin.

Hearing

Listen to the sounds around you. What is the loudest sound? And what is the quietest? Rub your fingers together near your ear. Is this sound loud or quiet?

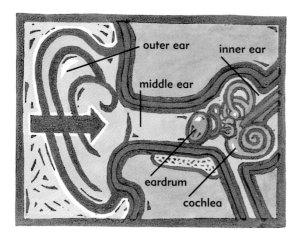

outer ear
inner ear
middle ear
eardrum
cochlea

▲ Your ears pick up sounds from the **sound waves** that travel through the air. The sound waves are received by the outer ear and are directed into the middle ear. Here, the sound waves **vibrate** the thin membrane of the eardrum. Tiny bones in the middle ear vibrate, causing movements in the liquid inside the **cochlea**. Nerves here change the movements into signals and send them to the brain. The liquid in the cochlea also helps your body to balance.

▼ Place rice or small sweets on a drum skin. Hold a baking tray above the drum and strike it. Sound waves will travel through the air, vibrating the drum skin and shaking the rice or sweets.

◀ Sounds can travel through solid objects, such as walls or the ground. Some Native Americans put their ear to the ground to listen for approaching riders.

▶ Dolphins communicate by sending sounds with a high **frequency** through the water. They judge distance by the echoes that return. Dolphins can see, hear and touch but cannot smell.

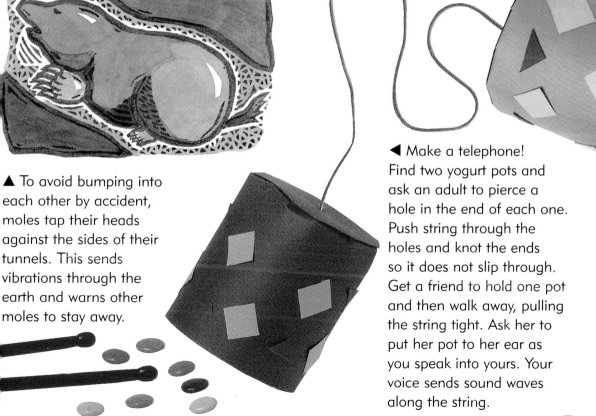

▲ To avoid bumping into each other by accident, moles tap their heads against the sides of their tunnels. This sends vibrations through the earth and warns other moles to stay away.

◀ Make a telephone! Find two yogurt pots and ask an adult to pierce a hole in the end of each one. Push string through the holes and knot the ends so it does not slip through. Get a friend to hold one pot and then walk away, pulling the string tight. Ask her to put her pot to her ear as you speak into yours. Your voice sends sound waves along the string.

Loud and soft

Many sounds are pleasant but some can cause harm. At a party or disco, the noise may be so great that you can later hear ringing in your ears. If so, your ears have suffered temporary damage.

▲ Large machinery used in industry, such as mining, or smaller equipment, such as some tractors or pneumatic drills, can produce deafening sound levels. Workers must wear heavy earphones to protect their ears. There are sound levels set by law in many countries. Too much noise present in the environment is called noise pollution.

▶ Not everyone enjoys listening to the same sounds. Your friend's favourite music may sound terrible to you! Some sounds are too high for people to hear, such as the sounds from dog whistles and some bird, insect and bat noises. Instead of hearing very low sounds, we feel them as rumbling vibrations.

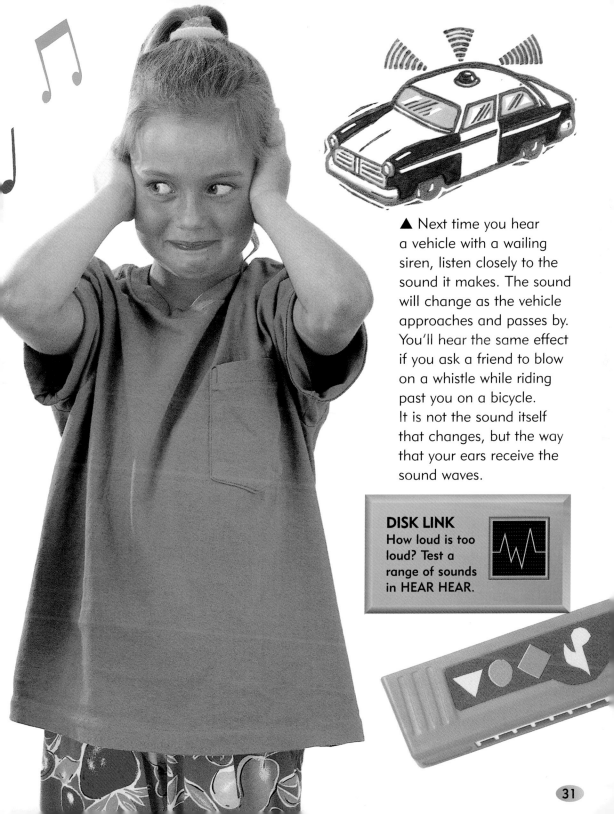

▲ Next time you hear
a vehicle with a wailing
siren, listen closely to the
sound it makes. The sound
will change as the vehicle
approaches and passes by.
You'll hear the same effect
if you ask a friend to blow
on a whistle while riding
past you on a bicycle.
It is not the sound itself
that changes, but the way
that your ears receive the
sound waves.

DISK LINK
How loud is too
loud? Test a
range of sounds
in HEAR HEAR.

Different worlds

Some people are born without the use of one or more senses, or their senses have been affected by an accident or illness. Often, their other senses become sharper.

▲ Many people wear contact lenses or spectacles. The extra lens changes the focus of their eyes. Short-sighted eyes cannot focus on distant objects. Long-sighted eyes cannot focus on objects that are close.

THE BRAILLE SYSTEM

CELL

A	B	C	D	E
F	G	H	I	J
K	L	M	N	O
P	Q	R	S	T
U	V	X	Y	Z

▲ In 1829, a Frenchman called Louis Braille created a system of reading and writing for the blind. **Braille** is a series of raised dots, read with the fingertips.

▶ As people grow older, their sense organs become less sensitive. They may need to wear spectacles or a hearing aid.

▲ Guide dogs act as eyes for their blind owners. They can signal danger, or tell their owner when to cross a busy road.

▼ People who are deaf can use language systems other than talking, such as signing with the hands and lip reading.

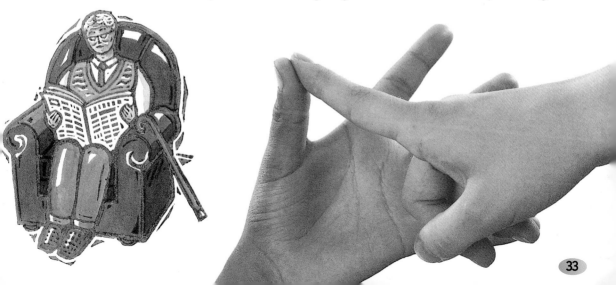

Glossary

Bacteria are tiny life forms. They can live almost anywhere – in the air, water or soil, on plants or animals, and on food or objects. Some types of bacteria are useful but others cause diseases.

roses

Braille is a written language used by blind people. It is made up of a series of raised dots that stand for letters and are read with the fingertips.

Brain is the control centre of the body. It receives information from the body's senses, stores memories, makes decisions and organises the actions of the muscles.

Cell is the smallest part of living matter. All living things are made up of cells.

Cochlea is a tube in the ear. It is filled with liquid and is lined with tiny hairs. Sound vibrations move the liquid, which touches the hairs. Each hair is attached to a nerve that sends a sound signal to the brain.

police car with siren

Cornea is a thin, clear layer that covers the front of the eyeball and the iris.

Cortex is the wrinkled layer of nerves covering the largest part of the brain.

Digest is to break down food and release its energy.

Focus is to make light rays meet, forming a clear image.

Frequency is the number of vibrations in a sound wave.

Glands produce chemical substances or help to remove waste products from the body. For example, there are sweat glands in the skin and tear glands near the eye.

Iris is the coloured part of the eye. It absorbs strong light and changes the size of the pupil.

Lens is the part of the eye that focuses light on to the retina. It is behind the iris.

Melanin is a pigment in the skin, hair and eyes. It helps to protect against sunburn.

Membrane is a very thin and delicate piece of body tissue.

Minerals are solid, non-living materials from the ground. Calcium, iron and coal are examples of minerals.

listening to vibrations

Mucus is a slimy substance that is produced to protect the delicate linings of the body. One type of mucus forms in your nose when you have a cold.

Muscles are large groups of cells that help the body to move and function. They are tough and stretchy.

Nerves are long, thin cells that run throughout the body. Some nerves carry messages from the senses to the brain. Others process these messages. And other nerves carry messages from the brain to the muscles, telling them what to do.

Pupil is the small, round hole in the front of the eye.

Retina is the area of light-sensitive cells at the back of the eye. It sends sight signals to the brain.

Saliva is the liquid produced in the glands of the cheeks and tongue. It moistens food, helping you to chew and swallow. Saliva also starts to break down food, making it easier for the body to digest.

Sweat is the salty liquid that is created by the skin to cool the body.

Sound waves are the vibrations that carry sounds through the air, water or solid objects.

Vibrate is to move rapidly, backwards and forwards. Sound travels as vibrations.

red and green spectacles

Work book

Work book

Loading your INTERFACT disk

INTERFACT is available on floppy disk and CD-ROM for both PCs with Windows and Apple Macs. Make sure you follow the correct instructions for the disk you have chosen and your type of computer. Before you begin, check the minimum specification (inside front cover).

CD-ROM INSTRUCTIONS

If you have a copy of INTERFACT on CD, you can run the program from the disk – you don't need to install it on your hard drive.

PC WITH WINDOWS 95

1. Put the disk in the CD drive
2. Open MY COMPUTER
3. Double click on the CD drive icon
4. Double click on the icon called SENSES

PC WITH WINDOWS 3.1 OR 3.11

1. Put the disk in the CD drive
2. Select RUN from the FILE menu in the PROGRAM MANAGER
3. Type **D:\SENSES** (Where D is the letter of your CD drive)
4. Press the RETURN key

APPLE MAC

1. Put the disk in the CD drive
2. Double click on the INTERFACT icon
3. Double click on the icon called SENSES

FLOPPY DISK INSTRUCTIONS

If you have a copy of INTERFACT on floppy disk, you must install the program on to your computer's hard drive before you can run it.

PC WITH WINDOWS 3.1 OR 3.11

To install INTERFACT:
1. Put the disk in the floppy drive
2. Select RUN from the FILE menu in the PROGRAM MANAGER
3. Type **A:\INSTALL** (Where A is the letter of your floppy drive)
4. Click OK – unless you want to change the name of the INTERFACT directory

To run INTERFACT:
Once the program has installed, open the INTERFACT group in the PROGRAM MANAGER and double click on the icon called SENSES

PC WITH WINDOWS 95

To install INTERFACT:
1. Put the disk in the floppy drive
2. Select RUN from the START menu
3. Type **A:\INSTALL** (Where A is the letter of your floppy drive)
4. Click OK – unless you want to change the name of the INTERFACT directory

To run INTERFACT:
Once the program has installed, open the START menu and select PROGRAMS then select INTERFACT and click on the icon called SENSES

APPLE MAC

To install INTERFACT:
1. Put the disk in the floppy drive
2. Double click on the icon called INTERFACT INSTALLER
3. Click CONTINUE
4. Click INSTALL – unless you want to change the name of the INTERFACT folder

To run INTERFACT:
Once the program has installed, open the INTERFACT folder and double click on the icon called SENSES

How to use INTERFACT

INTERFACT is easy to use.
First find out how to load the program
(see page 40) then read these simple
instructions and dive in!

You will find that there are lots of different features to explore. Use the controls on the right-hand side of the screen to select the one you want to play. You will see that the main area of the screen changes as you click on to different features.

For example, this is what your screen will look like when you play Top to Toe, where you can put Sam Sensitive's senses to the test. Once you've selected a feature, click on the main screen to start playing.

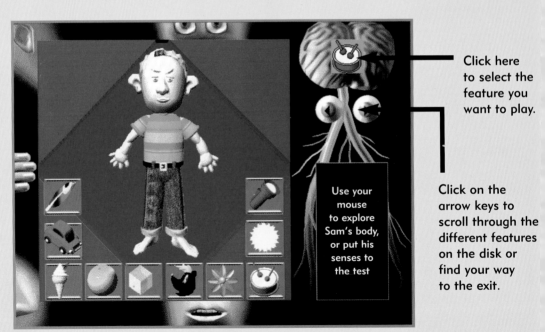

Click here to select the feature you want to play.

Use your mouse to explore Sam's body, or put his senses to the test

Click on the arrow keys to scroll through the different features on the disk or find your way to the exit.

This is the reading box where instructions and directions appear explaining what to do. Go to page 4 to find out what's on the disk.

DISK LINKS

When you read the book, you'll come across Disk Links. These show you where to find activities on the disk that relate to the page you are reading. Use the arrow keys to find the icon on screen that matches the one in the Disk Link.

DISK LINK
Should you always believe your eyes? Find out when you play EYE OPENERS.

BOOKMARKS

As you play the features on the disk, you'll bump into Bookmarks. These show you where to look in the book for more information about the topic on screen. Just turn to the page of the book shown in the Bookmark.

23

WORK BOOK

On pages 36-39 you'll find note pages to photocopy and use again and again. Use them to write down your own discoveries as you go through the book and the disk.

HOT DISK TIPS

● After you have chosen the feature you want to play, remember to move the cursor from the icon to the main screen before clicking on the mouse again.

● If you don't know how to use one of the on-screen controls, simply touch it with your cursor. An explanation will pop up in the reading box!

● Keep a close eye on the cursor. When it changes from an arrow ➔ to a hand ☞ click your mouse and something will happen.

● Any words that appear on screen in blue and underlined are 'hot'. This means you can touch them with the cursor for more information.

● Explore the screen! There are secret hot spots and hidden surprises to find.

Troubleshooting

If you have a problem with the INTERFACT disk, you should find the solution here. You can also call the helpline on 0171 684 4050. The lines are open from 10am to 5pm, Monday to Friday and calls are charged at normal rates. But remember to get permission from the person who pays the bill before you use the phone.

QUICK FIXES Run through these general checkpoints before consulting COMMON PROBLEMS (see opposite page).

QUICK FIXES **PC WITH WINDOWS 3.1 OR 3.11**

1 Check that you have the minimum specification: 386/33 Mhz, VGA colour monitor, 4 Mb of RAM.

2 Make sure you have typed in the correct instructions: a colon (:) not a semi-colon (;) and a back slash (\) not a forward slash (/). Also, do not use punctuation or put any spaces between letters.

3 It is important that you do not have any other programs running. Before you start **INTERFACT**, hold down the Control key and press Escape. If you find that other programs are open, click on them with the mouse, then click the End Task key.

QUICK FIXES **PC WITH WINDOWS 95**

1 Make sure you have typed in the correct instructions: a colon (:) not a semi-colon (;) and a back slash (\) not a forward slash (/). Also, do not use punctuation or put any spaces between letters.

2 It is important that you do not have any other programs running. Before you start **INTERFACT**, look at the task bar. If you find that other programs are open, click on them with the right mouse button and select Close from the pop-up menu.

APPLE MAC

1 Make sure that you have the minimum specification: 68020 processor, 640x480 colour display, system 7.0 (or a later version) and 4 Mb of RAM.

2 It is important that you do not have any other programs running. Before you start **INTERFACT**, click on the application menu in the top right-hand corner. Select each of the open applications and select Quit from the File menu.

COMMON PROBLEMS

Symptom: Cannot load disk.
Problem: There is not enough space available on your hard disk.
Solution: Make more space available by deleting old applications and programs you don't use until 6 Mb of free space is available.

Symptom: There is no sound (PCs only).
Problem: Your sound card is not Soundblaster compatible.
Solution: Configure sound settings to make them Soundblaster compatible (see your sound card manual for more information).

Symptom: Disk will not run.
Problem: There is not enough memory available.
Solution: *Either* quit other applications and programs (see Quick Fixes) *or* increase your machine's RAM by adjusting the Virtual Memory.

Symptom: Your machine freezes.
Problem: There is not enough memory available.
Solution: *Either* quit other applications and programs (see Quick Fixes) *or* increase your machine's RAM by adjusting the Virtual Memory.

Symptom: Graphics do not load or are of poor quality.
Problem: *Either* there is not enough memory available *or* you have the wrong display setting.
Solution: *Either* quit other applications and programs (see Quick Fixes) *or* make sure that your monitor control is set to 256 colours (MAC) or VGA (PC).

Symptom: Text does not fit neatly into boxes and 'hot' copy does not bring up extra information.
Problem: Standard fonts on your computer have been moved or deleted.
Solution: Re-install standard fonts. The PC version requires Arial; the Mac version requires Helvetica. See your computer manual for further information.

Index